NATIONAL
GEOGRAPHIC

Traveling Across Australia

Ming Tan

Contents

Australia

Australia is a **continent**. A continent is a very large area of land. There are seven continents in the world. Australia is an island continent. It is completely surrounded by water. It lies between the Pacific Ocean and the Indian Ocean.

Australia is also a country. It is the sixth largest country in the world. It is almost the size of the United States.

Australia is south of, or under, the **Equator**. That's why it is called the "land down under." Because of its location, the seasons in Australia are opposite to those in the United States. In Australia, it is winter in August and summer in January!

ATLANTIC
OCEAN

PACIFIC
OCEAN

EQUATOR

INDIAN
OCEAN

PACIFIC
OCEAN

AUSTRALIA

The People

The **Aboriginal people** have lived in Australia for more than 40,000 years. Long ago, the Aboriginal people lived in small groups. Each group was made up of several

Quandong fruit grows in the deserts of central Australia.

families. They hunted animals, such as kangaroos, emus, lizards, and fish. They ate the local plants, nuts, and fruits.

The Aboriginal people believe spiritual beings created the world. They call this the **Dreaming**. The stories of the Dreaming are told in songs, dances, and paintings.

This Aboriginal painting tells a story of the Dreaming.

The first European settlers arrived in Australia in 1788. They were English prisoners and their guards. The prisons in England were very crowded. Some of the English prisoners were sent to Australia for punishment.

In later years, immigrants began to arrive in Australia. Immigrants are people who choose to live in a new country. During the 1850s Gold Rush, many people migrated to Australia from England, China, and Ireland. They wanted to find gold and have a better life. After World War II, many people migrated from Greece and Italy.

Today, people come to live in Australia from countries all over the world.

The Coast

Australia has 17,366 miles (27,948 kilometers) of coastline. Most of the people in Australia live in the cities on the coast. People built the cities near the water so that they could ship goods in and out. The **harbors** of these coastal cities are large and perfect for big ships.

The city of Sydney is built on a large, busy harbor.

Sydney, the Largest City

Sydney is the largest and oldest city in Australia. It is the first place most people visit when they come to Australia. Every day hundreds of boats go in and out of the harbor. You see ferries, water taxis, and tour boats there.

AUSTRALIA

Sydney

The Great Barrier Reef

The Great Barrier Reef is the largest **coral reef** in the world. It is also one of the oldest living things in the world. How can a reef be alive?

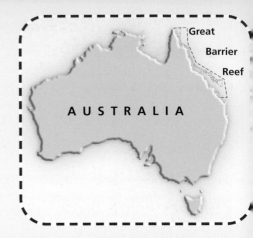

The reef is made up of small sea creatures called coral polyps. When a polyp dies, its skeleton stays on the ocean floor. New polyps grow on top of the skeletons. Layer after layer of reef builds over the years. Today, the reef stretches over 1,200 miles (1,930 kilometers).

About 400 different kinds of coral live in the Great Barrier Reef.

The reef is home to many colorful fish and coral.

More than 1,500 different kinds of fish live in the Great Barrier Reef. The fish are all colors. They look like rainbows swimming in the water. Many different kinds of shellfish, such as giant clams, live here, too.

Black marlins are very big fish. Some of the largest black marlins in the world live in the Great Barrier Reef. Humpback whales visit here, too. They come to have their calves in the warm waters.

The Daintree Rain Forest

Daintree rain forest

AUSTRALIA

The Daintree rain forest is on the northeast coast of Australia. It is the world's oldest tropical rain forest. It has been growing for more than 100 million years!

It is warm all year in the Daintree rain forest. There are only two seasons here. They are the "wet" and the "dry" seasons. It rains a lot in the wet season.

The Daintree rain forest is one of the wettest places in Australia. Most rain falls in the six months of the wet season.

The rain forest is a very special place. It has many plants and animals that don't live anywhere else. You can find tree kangaroos living in the rain forest! They have long, curved claws that help them climb and cling to trees.

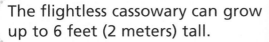
Tree kangaroos eat leaves.

Some dangerous animals live in the rain forest. The cassowary is a large bird that lives in the rain forest. Cassowaries can attack people. If you see one, do not run from it. Keep looking at the bird and back away slowly.

The flightless cassowary can grow up to 6 feet (2 meters) tall.

Monkey Mia

Australia has many, many beaches. There is a beach in Western Australia called Monkey Mia. There are no monkeys here. But there are dolphins. The dolphins swim in the shallow waters where people can feed them by hand. Sometimes the dolphins offer people fish they have caught in the sea!

Monkey Mia

AUSTRALIA

People can get close to dolphins at Monkey Mia.

The Outback

The land in the middle of Australia is far away from the cities on the coast. Australians call this vast area the **outback**. The outback is a hard place to live. The sun beats down on the land during the day. Most of the people living there earn money working on cattle stations or in mines.

Cattle Stations

In Australia, large farms in the outback are called stations. The beef cattle stations are huge. Because the land in the outback is very dry, the cattle need a large area to feed on.

Station hands use motorcycles to herd cattle in the outback.

The cattle stations are not close to any large cities or towns. When people get sick, they call the Royal Flying Doctor Service. A plane flies in, bringing a doctor to the sick person. Very sick people are flown to the nearest hospital.

Today, some of the cattle stations rent rooms to tourists who come to the outback. You can help round up the cattle. You can also swim in hot springs and see some amazing scenery and wildlife.

The Royal Flying Doctor Service is taking this baby home.

Mining

There are many mines in the outback of Australia. Lead, copper, silver, and iron ore are mined in the outback. Mining in the outback costs a great deal. The mines are far away from the cities. New roads have to be built to the mines. New towns also have to be built so that the mine workers have a place to live.

Gold is mined in Australia. Most gold comes from a place in the outback called Kalgoorlie-Boulder. People have been mining gold there since 1893. The Golden Mile at Kalgoorlie-Boulder is one of the richest goldfields in the world.

Kalgoorlie-Boulder has one of the largest open-cut mines in the world. It is called the "Golden Mile Super Pit."

This necklace is made from opal mined at Coober Pedy.

Australia is famous for the opals that are mined there. Opals are gemstones. They contain many different colors that flash out from a white or dark background. Opals are made into beautiful jewelry.

Almost all the world's opals come from Australia. Many of these opals are mined in an outback town called Coober Pedy. Anyone with a permit can look for opals there.

The Desert

Much of outback Australia is desert. There are two main types of desert in Australia. Gibber deserts are covered in stones called "gibbers." Sandy deserts are covered in **sand dunes**. Some of the sand dunes are over 100 feet (31 meters) high!

Wild camels roam the desert. The first camels were brought to Australia in 1840. They were used to help white settlers explore the outback. As people started to build roads, they used camels less. The camels were set free. Today, hundreds of thousands of wild camels live in the Australian desert.

The Simpson Desert is covered in sand dunes.

A favorite place for tourists to visit is Uluru. Uluru is a huge rock that is 1,132 feet (345 meters) tall. Uluru is a special place for the local Aboriginal people. Many stories of the Dreaming talk about Uluru.

Uluru is made of red sandstone.

The Bush

Australians call the country areas in between the cities and the outback, the **bush**. Many types of farming are done in the bush. One of the most important is sheep farming.

Sheep **shearing** is the biggest event of the year on a sheep farm. That is when the shearers cut the wool off the sheep. They use electric clippers to do this. Shearing is hard and tiring work. The fleece is cut off in one piece. Some sheep can give more than 15 pounds (7 kilograms) of fleece. That's a lot of wool!

The shearer holds the sheep still while he cuts off the fleece. The shearer works quickly and carefully.

Bush Animals

Koalas are one of the animals that live in the bush. Koalas spend most of their time in trees. They eat the leaves of eucalyptus trees. Koalas have pouches. A baby koala spends about six and a half months in its mother's pouch.

Koalas spend most of their time resting in trees.

The echidna is another animal that lives in the bush. Echidnas are small anteaters that are covered with spines. They can roll into a ball to protect themselves. Nothing can pick up this spiky ball!

Echidnas have strong claws that are good for digging.

A platypus is an animal that lives in streams in the bush. It is covered in fur and has a bill like a duck. A platypus lays its eggs in a burrow. The mother looks after the babies until they are big enough to come out.

The platypus searches for food with its duck-like bill.

The most famous Australian bush animal is the kangaroo. A picture of a kangaroo is often used as a **symbol** of Australia. Kangaroos hop on their strong hind legs. Baby kangaroos are very tiny when they are born. They stay in their mother's pouch for about eight months.

Baby kangaroos are called joeys.

A Great Place to Visit!

Many people visit Australia each year. They go to see the harbor cities, the lush rain forest, and the beautiful beaches. Some people travel into the outback to visit a cattle station. Or they catch a plane across the desert to see Uluru. There are plenty of things to see and do in Australia.

Bondi Beach in Sydney is a popular place for tourists to visit in summer.

Glossary

Aboriginal people   the first people to live in Australia

bush   country areas in Australia

continent   a very large area of land

coral reef   a long ridge of coral found near the surface of the sea; coral is made from the skeletons of tiny sea creatures

Dreaming   spiritual beliefs of Aboriginal people

Equator   an imaginary line that separates the northern and southern halves of Earth

harbor   a place for ships to shelter

outback   the land in the middle of Australia that is far away from the cities on the coast

sand dune   a big hill of sand

shearing   to cut the wool off sheep

symbol   a picture used to stand for something

Index